Wicker

DESIGN

Mary Whitesides

Gibbs Smith, Publisher
Salt Lake City

First Edition

07 06 05 04 03   5 4 3 2 1

Published by
Gibbs Smith, Publisher
P.O. Box 667
Layton, Utah 84041

Orders: (1-800) 748-5439
www.gibbs-smith.com

Edited by Jennifer Grillone
Designed and produced by Ron Stucki
Printed and bound in Hong Kong

Library of Congress Cataloging-in-Publication Data

Whitesides, Mary.
Wicker design / Mary Whitesides.—1st ed.
p. cm.
ISBN 1-58685-244-2
1. Wicker furniture. I. Title.
NK2712.7.W48 2003
684.1'06—dc21
2003007895

Contents

Acknowledgments

I would like to thank Gibbs Smith, Publisher for the opportunity to create this book. It has been a fascinating journey into one of the most creative processes in furniture making. Because of the weaving techniques used in making wicker, shapes and forms are an endless possibility.

I thank Leslie Curtis of Curtis Antiques for her assistance in locating some of the most unusual pieces of wicker available on the antique market. Her vast knowledge on this subject is a great contribution to the book.

Henry and Maxine Speski of Connecticut Antique Wicker were most gracious in sharing forty years of treasured photos collected throughout their time dedicated to the antique wicker business.

Ken Bauer of Bauer International carries forward a passion for plantation woven furniture. He has reproduced and updated Asian wicker for the contemporary market. I appreciate his expertise and willingness to share information.

I thank Darcy Forman and Lisa Frudden of Palecek for time spent locating photos and answering questions. Palecek has one of the most comprehensive and innovative lines of wicker furniture in today's home furnishings market.

Martin Kuckly of Kuckly Associates, interior designer Gina Robinson, and Virginia Goshi of Lifestyle Interiors all took a chance on a stranger and an out-of-the-blue phone call. I thank them for their response to my request for photographs of their work.

And lastly, thank you to my editor Jennifer Grillone who always provides great insight into such books as *Wicker Design*.

Introduction

The art of weaving furniture from vines or stems is the oldest craft in the world. It dates back thousands of years and is still current today. Wicker is not a particular material in and of itself, but a classification of furniture and accessories woven from any one of a variety of materials. The true beauty of wicker is that it is made into functional works of art.

The word *wicker* is taken from the Scandinavian words *wika*, meaning "bend," and *vikker*, meaning "willow." Because of the craftsman's ability to bend and mold vines into endless shapes and forms, wicker furniture is a delightful medium that captures the designer's imagination. Fascinating pieces of wicker furniture come from throughout the ages; they tell stories of whimsy, comfort, fashion, and durability. Wicker is a dynamic medium that always has a place in the home.

1

The Art of
Making Wicker

Natural fibers are the inspiration for the craft of weaving wicker. Different climates provide the craftsman with different raw materials. In cold climates, willow twigs, roots, wood strips, wild grasses, and rushes are used. These materials give furniture a coarse, rustic look. In warmer climates, palm leaves, cane, reeds, grasses, and rattan are made into furniture. These fibers give the finished product a more refined look. The most popular material for wicker is stripped rattan.

Rattan, a native plant in Southeast Asia, is a climbing palm with a thin, hard bark and a solid core. Cane, the pared outer

*Right: The hand-weaving process for making wicker furniture is an art form. This wooden frame provides a sort of loom for woven rattan peel. The fibers are soaked for flexibility and are strengthened through the drying process. Small hairs are singed off when dry to smooth the surface. **Opposite:** Artesanias de Colombia's designers use clean, sleek lines to define this contemporary lounge. The back is ergonomically correct and is comfortable without a cushion. A side table on wheels is convenient for serving tea, coffee, or finger foods on the patio.*

surface, is most commonly used in the woven seats and backs of chairs. Reed, the soft inner pith, is used in weaving intricate and complicated patterns. Rattan grows in long, slender, uniform stems as it reaches for light in the rain forest. It can grow up to six hundred feet long and has a lengthwise grain, making it flexible. Rattan differs from wood in that it doesn't splinter; it differs from bamboo in that it has a solid core. Wicker rattan is extremely durable and rugged, making it a practical choice for furniture. It is one of the strongest natural materials available and can last a lifetime if properly maintained.

To prepare rattan for use, the stems and outer protective layers are removed. Poles are fumigated and then extruded through a machine to

*Left: The open weave on wicker furniture was first introduced during the early 1900s to save time and money in manufacturing. The look of it became very popular and started a new trend in wicker furniture. Here a combination of closed and open weave makes a unique chair. **Below:** Weaving natural fibers can be as intricate and complicated as knitting a sweater. Here is an example of wicker that actually resembles a sweater stitch.*

Rattan pole is peeled and bundled in preparation for the weaving process. Only a few fibers are soaked at a time. The pliable rattan peel is woven on a metal frame that provides the structure and shape for a wicker dining room chair. This artisan is weaving a graphic pattern on the chair back. (See completed chair on page 14.)

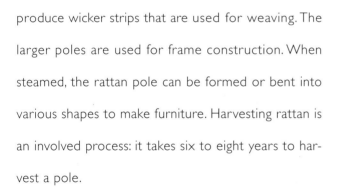

produce wicker strips that are used for weaving. The larger poles are used for frame construction. When steamed, the rattan pole can be formed or bent into various shapes to make furniture. Harvesting rattan is an involved process: it takes six to eight years to harvest a pole.

Hand-weaving wicker furniture is a time-consuming, skill-intensive process. First, the reeds or strips are soaked over a period of time to soften them and make them pliable for weaving. The weaver uses a series of tools such as scissors, needle-nose pliers, wire cutters, awls, hammers, and clippers. At a workbench, a series of stakes is set up for the base; a foot border insures the base will not separate from the stakes. The product is then woven in a series of three-piece fibers that act as base, filler, and top; fibers are braided to complete the item. Once completed, wicker must dry for twenty-four hours. This allows the fibers to shrink and tighten to form the final product. Tiny hairs and imperfections are singed off with a torch and rough areas are smoothed out with a final sanding. Furniture can then be lacquered, oiled, painted, or stained. The selection of a finish further individualizes the piece. For example, lacquer can give a piece an oriental look, while a stain and a coat of linseed oil can create a country feel. Wicker can also be painted to suit the individual whim of the owner.

Today it is rare for wicker furniture to be completely handwoven. As early as the 1800s, the industry searched for methods to cut costs on the labor-intensive weaving techniques. One solution was the introduction of wood frames. Instead of weaving the entire piece of furniture from rattan fibers, wood frames were used and fibers were woven

Left: Skilled hands weave a rattan peel detail for a piece of furniture. The strength of the wooden frame is reinforced by fiber-wrapped corners. The craftsman works quickly and precisely to complete the section before the soaked fibers dry. Opposite: Wicker made of natural rattan pole soaked and bent into simple shapes was popular at the turn of the century. Consumers were tired of busy curlicues and wanted straightforward, uncomplicated designs such as these "snowshoe" chairs.

around the frames. The weight-bearing portion of such products as serving

trays, baby bassinets, and shelves were also made of wood with wicker as an

accent. In addition to cutting down weaving time, wood frames increase the

durability of furniture.

Importing reed from Asia also became cost prohibitive. By the 1920s,

manufacturers had developed a new fiber called fiber reed or art fiber. To

make fiber reed, paper is twisted around wire and woven onto a hardwood

frame. The advent of National Park lodges during this period sparked creative

Above left: The earliest known craft is wicker. Baskets were made of wicker thousands of years ago and depictions of them are found at archeological sites. Here baskets made of willow have the strength of any wooden vessel. These heavy-duty baskets are sturdy enough to tote canned foods, tools, or a picnic lunch. Above right: A combination of fibers gives craftsmen the ability to create interesting patterns. This oriental pattern is influenced by early Asian designs first adapted into Victorian wicker furniture and imported for the homes of the neuveau riches. Opposite: Innovative designers from Artesanias de Colombia look at form and function in a new way. This wicker bench doubles as a coffee table. The massive legs add not only physical strength but visual panache as well.

architecture known as Park Architecture. Art fiber furniture first appeared on the porches of these grand structures and became synonymous with the design of this time period. Woven paper furniture is surprisingly durable, cool, clean, and economical.

Innovative designers and craftsmen discovered that a combination of materials was not only practical but provided endless opportunities for creativity and design. A wide range of designs emerged with this concept. Wood made the product sturdy; rush and reed allowed for elaborate decorative designs; cane functioned well as a seat material because of its resilient and

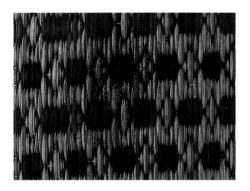

Left: The art and refinement of making wicker furniture has evolved to that of fine woven fabric. The pattern woven into this wicker furniture can be compared to quality gabardine. Combining bent rattan poles with leather and wicker garners the best of several design periods. The luxurious cowhide cushions assure comfort to suit a contemporary life-style.

flexible qualities. The best examples of the use of wood in wicker can be seen in turn-of-the-century furniture. Manufacturers expanded their production to include tables, desks, bookshelves, sewing tables, and infant changing tables.

In the 1950s, the look of rattan was often duplicated by round sections of steamed bentwood. These economical substitutions were stained and charred to appear that they had the natural notches left by branches. If you are considering purchasing a vintage '50s piece, you should inspect the frame to make sure it is constructed of authentic rattan.

Natural sea grass, royal palm, rush, raffia, abaca, and junco fibers are some of the innovative materials being used to make contemporary wicker armchairs, footstools, tables, and benches. Sea grass and palm fibers have a soft quality that rattan does not. Many people who love natural fiber furniture prefer the comfort of these chairs to the hard-edged Victorian furniture pieces. Furniture using these materials is manufactured in Asian countries where such fibers are prolific.

Other countries use fibers for making wicker that are readily available, and in so doing perform an ecological service as well. In Colombia, for

Above: Applied woven patterns first appeared on wicker during the 1920s and continued into the Art Deco period. This is an easy way to distinguish between periods. **Opposite:** *Using wooden frames allowed designers and manufacturers to create new products from wicker. Bassinets and changing tables with solid wood bottoms have now become classics. With a mattress and soft blankets, these two original pieces are still appropriate for a newborn's nursery.*

instance, junco fiber grows so fast it virtually chokes out lakes. Indigenous people harvest this fiber, thereby saving the lake, and use the fiber as an economical material for their craft. Junco is pliable enough to weave into intricate forms and is strong enough to make a product such as a basket or hamper efficient and substantial. Junco fiber is smooth to the touch and rich in color.

Diverse fibers, distinct forms, and a broad and varied collection of designs create

an unlimited number of wicker-style furniture pieces. Wicker is suited to whatever the current trend in interior design might be. With its wide range of materials and the many different methods used to create it, wicker is indeed a versatile product. It comes in many styles to meet a wide range of personal tastes. Whether you have a preference for the Rococo style of the Victorian era, the sleek simple lines of the Arts & Crafts movement, or the malleable plush lines of a contemporary chair, a piece of woven furniture can be found to enhance your home.

Painted furniture became popular when consumers took it upon themselves to paint and refresh their wicker. It is a good way to personalize a space and it is not hard to achieve the look you want. This unusually bold, deep pink chair complements the umber-colored walls of a bungalow in the Andes Mountains of Colombia.

The Art of Making Wicker   *31*

2

Styles of Wicker

Wicker has been used throughout the ages. It dates back to ancient Egypt and China, and is still in use in modern America. Wicker was very popular during the Victorian period in England and America in the late 1800s and early 1900s. The furniture designs of this period included fanciful shapes and elaborate scrollwork. In the 1920s, '30s and '40s, the Arts & Crafts movement in America produced wicker furniture with simple forms and dense weaves combined with open weaves. Art Deco style spanned the 1920s to the 1950s. This style used an open framework for wicker furniture, using full pieces of rattan wrapped with leather or cane strips. Contemporary wicker features combination weaves and raw materials.

PHOTO © HENRY SPESKI

Right: An early Victorian chair by Heywood Bros. has rolled arms and elaborate birdcage designs on the front of the legs. Spools and scallops embellish the skirt while a spiderweb weave flanked by pinwheels defines the back. This is a gentleman's chair sized to suit a male person. **Opposite:** *While the rest of a home may be formal, the sunroom begs to be casual. There is no better way to invite a guest to relax than a deep-seated wicker armchair.*

Victorian Wicker

A major defining style of the United States is found in the Victorian era of the late 1800s and early 1900s. A time of elegance and prosperity, the Victorian period produced homes that became places to showcase wealth for the newly rich. Carefully staged social affairs gave a flamboyant hostess the chance to display her latest acquisitions. Many furnishings installed in these grand mansions were imported from Europe.

New wealth brought the opportunity of world travel, and socialites were fascinated by the allure of the orient. Highly lacquered oriental wicker became quite popular in England and filtered into American homes as well. Wicker began to be used as a means to decorate with a more open, airy feeling; it lent a more casual feel to a room, providing an opportunity to relax in the midst of a house that was mainly stiff and formal. This was very popular with the leisurely rich. Because wicker was handwoven during this period, it was very

Right: A typical Victorian setting is at once reminiscent of your grandmother's parlor or the comfortable country-style interior many prefer in a second home. Delicate lace pillows are the perfect complement to the intricate Rococo-style back on this Victorian wicker chair.
Opposite: The Victorian era garnered design ideas from many different periods. The Rococo style became a favorite interpretation in wicker furniture during the 1800s. The ornate curlicue motif is found on numerous wicker pieces such as this perambulator. They are works of art and greatly valued in the antique market.

*Left: This chair is a good example of the Rococo influence on wicker crafts-manship. **Above:** Small parlor benches, vanity benches, and occasional benches were popular through the late 1800s and on into the early 1900s. The shapes are Turkish in design and are enhanced and embellished at the whim of the artisan. **Opposite:** Sue Balmforth creates a beautiful outdoor room, complete with pergola, vines, and even a chandelier. She chooses wicker furniture to maintain the ambience she desires.*

expensive, so it became a status symbol for those who owned it. Wicker also captured the exotic oriental look popular in the 1890s.

The Victorians loved to combine styles with an unusual mix of traditional and progressive designs, which were taken from numerous motifs from different periods, including Rococo, Classical, Elizabethan Gothic, Chinese, and Italian Renaissance. Influenced by this wide range of styles, wicker became a natural medium in which to develop different shapes and designs. Using this fiber, craftsmen and designers could develop the style they wanted. In the 1850s, New York designer John Topf revived the French Rococo style of the seventeenth and eighteenth centuries in wicker using motifs such as curlicues, C-scrolls, and cabriole legs.

In 1850, Cyrus Wakefield noticed a stack of rattan poles on a ship docked in a Boston harbor and wondered at the properties and possibilities of such a material. He started the Wakefield Rattan Company, which made baskets and furniture. This fueled the craze for wicker in the Victorian era to new heights.

Heywood Bros, the largest wooden chair company in the United States,

PHOTO © DEBRA MACFARLANE, BOUNTIFUL

Above: This Turkish bench is combined with the Rococo trend of the Victorian era. These benches were so popular that the consumers purchased them as fast as they could be produced.
Right: This simple plant stand has very little ornamentation, which was the preferred style of the consumer in the early 1920s. *Opposite: Martin Kuckly uses two reproduction Victorian chairs to add whimsy to a formal dining room. The rolled arms extending to the back, spools woven into the open back, and flared skirt supporting the legs all pay homage to early American wicker design.*

invented a loom in the 1840s that could weave cane and install seats on chairs. This dramatically cut the cost and time involved in making handwoven wicker furniture. Heywood also invented a machine that could bend wood remarkably well. The machine caught the attention of Francis Thonet, who invented the famous bentwood rocker. Wakefield and Heywood became fierce competitors, and the competition considerably lowered prices for woven furniture. In the early 1900s, prices for chairs ranged from a popular reed rocker at $2.99 to an upholstered rocker at $10.95. A three-piece sofa set sold for as much as $25.00. The two companies merged in 1897 and became known as the Heywood Wakefield Company. The company ultimately monopolized the industry through the 1920s.

By the 1880s, the Victorian wicker business reached an unprecedented high. The Heywood Wakefield Company produced thousands of innovative designs. Wicker was now available to all economic levels and served a functional aspect in daily life. The company produced such new items as gentlemen's chairs with oversized seats, large arms, high backs, and thick, intricate patterns. They also offered ladies' chairs, which were smaller in size—dainty with a

Below left: As craftsmen and designers began to broaden the spectrum of their product, tables, bassinets, trays, and tea carts were introduced. The addition of wood foundations, such as tray bottoms and tabletops, were used for stability and strength.

Left: Perambulators were a means of showing off a newborn baby. Many families strolled along main avenues of their hometown to parade their offspring. The buggy was as much on display as the child during Victorian times, but became secondary during the 1920s when designs changed to much cleaner, simpler lines. **Above:** The ever-changing shape of the bench lent itself to treasure hunts for the consumer. This bench combines the Turkish shape, the interwoven graphic patterns of the '20s Arts & Crafts movement, and the curlicues of the Rococo period. The bench seats two and was used in front of a fireplace.

Top left: *This sweepback chair, manufactured by Heywood Bros., is known as a reception chair. The rare intricate pinwheel design looks as delicate as lace but has survived for over a hundred years.* **Top right:** *This one-of-a-kind Victorian frame has over a hundred curlicues.* **Bottom left:** *This ladies' armchair, restored to its original natural wicker finish by Henry Speski of Connecticut Antique Wicker, was once painted white by a consumer. It is embellished with orange trim and dual color stick-and-ball construction.* **Bottom right:** *This photographer's chair was used as a prop in a photo studio and was specifically designed for portrait sittings.*

Right: Precise and closely woven, this scallop-backed chair would be impossible to make today. The skill and patience have been lost. The stain on the chair is in mint condition and not one fiber is out of place. *Far right:* Small parlor chairs with rolled backs, such as this one, were used as space savers. They can be moved about with ease and used wherever extra seating is required. *Below:* This whimsical love seat is a garden delight with two large flowers forming the back. The wooden frame filled with cane ensures solid seating. It was manufactured in 1870 by Heywood Bros.

delicate weave. The product line expanded further into conversation chairs, where young lovers could talk discretely without touching, and a special one-sided chair called a photographer's chair, suited to the needs of studios taking formal portraits.

Wicker was regarded as sanitary, easily cleaned, and lightweight. It's no surprise, then, that wicker children's furniture was introduced. Elaborately woven perambulators with scroll patterns and fancy parasols allowed a proud couple to stroll around the neighborhood showing off their baby. The first known piece of wicker in the United States was a child's crib that came from England on the Mayflower, and new crib designs, as well as changing tables and rocking chairs, were developed. Wicker furniture made decorating a child's nursery whimsical as well as practical. Fanciful rooms for babies are traditionally decorated in wicker furniture even today.

With its artistic lines, originality, and natural fiber, wicker brings a

Far left: A Victorian rocker has rolled arms that reach from the seat to the high back. An artistic cornucopia design complements a web of curlicues.
Left: This plant stand is called a Taboré. The wooden frame is connected by a paisley-like wicker pattern.
Opposite: Elegant country classic interiors mix beautifully with wicker furniture. People can sit comfortably in broad seats with cushions, without sinking too deeply. Easing in and out of the chairs is a breeze.

PHOTOS © HENRY SPESKI

Above left: *This is an Ordway platform rocker. The arms curve gently up the back, which dramatically dips in the center as a headrest.* *Above right:* *The seat of this chair began as a footstool. The Wakefield Company added a fancy high back to create a low-seated chair.* *Left:* *This natural wicker perambulator was used for an older child who could sit upright.*

warm, homey feeling to a room. Victorian wicker can find a place in any room in the house; however, sunrooms, parlors, front porches, and patios are the classic places to find an ensemble of Victorian wicker pieces. Furniture leaving the factories in Victorian times had a natural or lacquered finish, but people who wanted more colorful options began to take liberties by painting wicker to suit their own needs.

Top left: *An oval table from the Victorian era is difficult to find. This one has a wooden frame with a cane top and bottom shelf. Note the elaborate bird cage legs.* ***Bottom left:*** *A simple side table is dressed up with pineapple legs.* ***Above right:*** *Themed chairs became an artistic challenge for the craftsmen. This guitar chair was obviously meant to appeal to a musician.*

Arts & Crafts Wicker

After enjoying nearly a half-century of prosperity, the Victorian wicker industry began to falter when consumer taste turned to simple, straight lines. The shift in style was influenced by the writings and philosophy of the Arts & Crafts movement in England. Interest in wicker and natural fibers as economic, lightweight materials remained, but the ornate Victorian curlicues

*Below: Karpin Furniture Company of Chicago manufactured this kidney-shaped sofa in 1920. Manufacturers took their cue from the consumer and began offering painted furniture. This sofa was first painted with a gold base, then painted blue and the surface wiped to achieve a dual tone effect. **Opposite:** Brown was rarely used on wicker furniture before the 1920s, when clean lines, open work, and simple styles became popular. A small secretary's desk and chair provided a new direction in wicker design.*

PHOTO © HENRY SPESKI

Above: *Sue Balmforth of the antique store Bountiful in Los Angeles has created the ultimate romantic outdoor room. These mission-style wicker chairs add a poetic and capricious element to the space.* **Left:** *A quixotic tea cart such as this is a delight for serving guests afternoon tea. The cart is made of a wooden frame and has legs that are wrapped in rattan peel. It also has a removable glass tray. Made in 1915.*

Top right: This simple, open-weave dining chair is from the Arts & Crafts period. *Middle right:* Open work such as is shown on this rocker was originally designed to save time and money in the weaving process. The Lloyd Loom Co. invented machinery to do the job. *Bottom right:* Art fiber was another way manufacturers looked to cut the cost of importing rattan. This chair is constructed of paper-wrapped wire and was used as Park Lodge furniture in the 1930s. *Below:* The Chinese-red color on this dressing table reflects the Asian influence that was so popular at the turn of the century. The simplicity of design is in direct contrast to the earlier Rococo pieces.

were too much for the new, sleek design sense.

European designers and manufacturers led the way in design with stylized geometric wicker patterns. For the first time in thousands of years, the basic principals of wicker were abandoned. Flat seats with upholstery were used with wicker. Imported angular designs introduced into the market by Austrian firms

Left: During the 1920s, The Dryad Company in Europe hired designers to change the face of wicker. The table shown here has a flared base that was directly influenced by the new direction they created. Below left: The open, airy weave of this Bar Harbor sofa suggests a casual, relaxed atmosphere, inviting a guest to enjoy the comforts of home. Found at Bountiful antique store in Los Angeles. Below right: Original Bar Harbor wicker is in high demand by collectors. The Arts & Crafts movement of the early 1900s directly influenced the style and design on pieces like this lounge. Bar Harbor—style furniture is still manufactured today.

Top: *During the Arts & Crafts movement, wicker furniture became more comfortable as upholstered cushions were added. This Karpin Furniture Company ensemble has springs in the seats and cushions. The multiple diamond patterns add to the antique value of the set.* **Bottom left:** *Lampshades of the Arts & Crafts period were commonly lined in silk. This one has the original fabric with silk fringe. From Connecticut Antique Wicker.* **Bottom right:** *This Bar Harbor piece is rare when found in natural wicker as this is. The earth tones blend perfectly with the natural stonework on the patio.*

Right: This is a wingback Bar Harbor chair by Jenkin Felps Company, who produced high-end chairs. Note the magazine rack on the arms. *Far right:* A simple sofa table is made interesting when surrounded by an open weave adornment. *Below:* A very simple but popular Bar Harbor set.

PHOTO © HENRY SPESKI

PHOTO © MARY WHITESIDES

PHOTO © HENRY SPESKI

PHOTO © HENRY SPESKI

Above: These chairs of the Arts & Crafts period are trimmed out in braid and colored gray, making them much sought after as a set. They are sized and shaped for comfort; one is a rocker, the other a chair.
Right: A mission-style chair is updated with a striped ticking upholstery.

PHOTO © MARY WHITESIDES

were widely accepted by the American public. An English firm, the Dryad Company, was influenced by the new Austrian designs and employed a master basket-maker to create a completely new form in wicker. The shaped chair he developed had a skirt that flared to the floor, large sweeping arms, and a molded seat allowing comfort without upholstery.

European imports were taking over the wicker business, and American

Top: *Highly influenced by the French Napoleonic-style, this love seat has serpentine legs, and rolled arms and back.* **Left:** *Henry Speski of Connecticut Antique Wicker labels this chair the crème de la crème of the Victorian era. With the triple "X" weave and magazine rack arms, it is worth between $2,500 and $3,500 to a collector.* **Below:** *The flat box weave on this oval coffee table reflects the sleek lines demanded by the consumer of the Arts & Crafts movement.*

Right: The heart-shaped back of this puffed armchair creates a wingback effect. Note the convenient pockets on the inside of the arm. A Heywood Wakefield piece. **Far right:** A floor lamp with an "Eiffel Tower" base is a blue-label Heywood Wakefield piece manufactured in Chicago. The shade is trimmed in silk fringe. **Below:** The 1920s designs of the Dryad Company influenced this reproduction table. The flared base and substantial tabletop girth are key elements in this style of design, which crossed over to the Art Deco period.

PHOTO © HENRY SPESKI

PHOTO © HENRY SPESKI

PHOTO © MARY WHITESIDES

*Above left: Known as the "Eiffel Tower" table lamp, this piece was popular between 1920–30. **Above right:** Manufactured by the Jenkins Felps Company, this men's armchair is big with a high back to comfortably accommodate the male figure. Many companies tried to copy this chair but couldn't duplicate its strength and durability. **Below:** A rare red-and-black Heywood Wakefield table, this piece was painted at the factory after the consumer established the fad.*

companies were slow to catch on. To reduce the cost of the closely woven product coming out of Europe, the Cape Cod chair became popular. Following the sleek, clean lines of mission style, this chair has an airy, diamond-shaped

weave and features side pockets. This style is now widely known as Bar Harbor and is still the best-selling style of wicker.

The Heywood Wakefield Company started designing furniture in the popular mission style after being influenced by Stickley's interpretation of wicker furniture. Even though Heywood and Wakefield started this style for wicker, Marshal B. Lloyd found a way to manufacture the same style in half the time. He invented a machine in the 1920s that wove man-made fiber out of chemically treated, twisted paper that was stiffened with glue. This paper, called art fiber or fiber reed, could be transferred directly from his patented "Lloyd Loom" and fitted directly onto frames. Art fiber eliminated the need to import expensive natural fibers. The plainer, less expensive Park Lodge designs that Lloyd introduced caught on and sent the wicker industry in a new direction. Heywood and Wakefield took quick notice of the trend and bought the Lloyd Manufacturing Co., which continued to enjoy prosperous sales throughout the '20s. By the 1930s, however, synthetic wicker had lost its appeal.

Below left: An excellent example of the "X" weave technique after open weave furniture became popular. The love seat has stick-and-ball construction with a pressed cane seat. Made by Heywood Bros. Below right: An oval side table with modified cabriole legs has a wooden tabletop with a square shelf. The color was unusual for the time period. Found at Leslie Curtis Antiques, Los Angeles.

These bar stools and chairs are influenced by the Art Deco period. The full-size rattan pole construction is bound at the corners with peeled strips for strength. The circular pattern on the back is Asian influenced.

Art Deco Wicker

The industrial age ushered in the geometric designs of Art Deco, which were interpreted in wicker by sweeping shapes. Art Deco wicker often used an open framework with full pieces of rattan wrapped with leather or cane strips. The simple, functional line of Art Deco chairs was greatly influenced by the Dryad chairs. Diamond patterns commonly found on the backs and skirts of Art Deco wicker chairs and sofas were stained for contrast and to show the graphics of the times. This was also an era of American Indian motifs, which came from the popularity of Indian trade blankets, manufactured by Beacon Blanket Company and Pendleton Blanket Company. The new-style sofas and chairs relied heavily on upholstered seats for comfort and had inner spring systems rather than precisely rounded woven seats.

A number of new products were introduced during this period. Chaise longues, called wicker couches, emerged—with shapes

*The oval side table pictured here is on the cusp of change between the Arts & Crafts and Art Deco periods. Simplicity is still preferred, but the style begins to change with the bold use of the entire rattan pole. Interior designers would select a table like this as an accent piece to add texture and warmth to an eclectic mix of furniture.*

PHOTO © MARY WHITESIDES

Styles of Wicker **61**

that varied from a perfectly flat surface to a rounded raised head support. Such a Chaise longue commonly had no padding. This furniture was reminiscent of what might be found on a steamer ship bound for the Orient. Another product was the tea cart on wheels, which facilitated afternoon tea. Tea carts had a removable serving tray on top that conveniently lifted off for serving.

The Lloyd loom made it possible to manufacture close-weave wicker similar to the expensive handcrafted wicker imported from Europe. Innovative

Opposite: Graphic design is the byword of the Art Deco period, and this is no exception in the wicker furniture business. Here, a very simple table is accented with circular leg braces. The open look is inviting and uncluttered. Above: Stick wicker is rarely found in the antique market. Manufactured in the 1930s, its production was limited because of loss of interest in the market. It is now highly sought after. These pieces with the original bark cloth are in mint condition.

items like library tables, lamps, china cabinets, and even porch swings flooded the market. An entirely new look, called stick furniture, was made possible by these machines and this new design enjoyed a brief surge of popularity in the 1930s. The Will Rogers Estate has a library completely furnished in stick furniture made of exposed pole rattan that was upholstered in Beacon blankets.

After World War II, a renewed interest in rattan furniture took place with the new, wide-open floor plans that were appearing in homes. Because the

new look in rattan was light and airy, and still had elements of simplicity and tradition, it coincided with this fresh beginning in home design. Multiple rods of steam-bent rattan were bonded and shaped into loops and curves to become sculptured armchairs, sofas, dressers, footstools, and coffee tables. The furniture is molded, shaped, and bound at intervals for strength and interest. Chairs in the Art Deco period were given such names as double rainbow, square pretzel, and fan arm.

*Below left: A painted version of Dryad–influenced furniture, the chipped paint finish on this piece is a valuable find in the antique market. **Below right:** Beds were seldom made of wicker, so this single bed is unusual. It has the graphic design indicative of the transition between Arts & Crafts and Art Deco. It is difficult to distinguish the exact date of many pieces of wicker furniture because of crossover in design. **Opposite:** Wicker lounges like this one were found on ship decks of luxury liners. A blanket folded on the chair provided warmth and comfort to ship passengers.*

Above: *Wicker lounges first appeared in the early 1900s in an effort to expand the product available in the wicker industry. Today, wicker lounges are still a very popular choice for garden, patio, and porch settings. The ribbed weave on this lounge, high fanned back, broad arms, and graphic diamond-shaped knit within the rattan fabric defines the Art Deco period.* ***Opposite:*** *Large tropical prints known as bark cloth were popular in the 1950s. Three rattan poles are wrapped at intervals for strength. The triple pole structure gives visual substance to a chair like this. The infinity loop along the bottom edge of the ottoman is a good example of the flexible qualities of rattan.*

*Above left: A square wicker table reflects the geometric silhouettes of the industrial age. Art Deco changed the face of furniture design. **Above right:** In an effort to save a dying interest in woven furniture, stick wicker was invented. This look was only moderately successful and resulted in limited production. In today's market, these pieces are sought after.*

Natural rattan poles have rings where the exposed joints of removed branches add textural interest. Imitations were deftly made by the invention of Marshal B. Lloyd's machine that was capable of bending wood into shapes so that it had areas resembling these joints. The faux joints were stained and charred to resemble notches left by branches. Although the furniture had a decidedly tropical look, it could be found in many homes across the United

States. A bold print fabric called bark cloth, that was most often used for draperies, soon came to be the preferred cushion fabric for rattan furniture. Examples of rattan furniture from the 1950s can still be found all over Europe and the United States.

Right: *Graphic designs inspired by Native American patterns were used in a broad spectrum of design work during the 1940s. Wicker furniture was no exception.* **Below left:** *A deep upholstered seat brings balance and proportion to the arched back and flat arms on a Deco rocker. The ever-expanding version of graphic design is intricately woven into the back of the chair, and it trims the arched shape.* **Below right:** *Three square boxes generate a graphic steppe pattern on this Art Deco planter.*

Above: *Wicker that is woven in a dense, closed weave covers a wooden-frame chair like fabric. The high back is curved to hug the occupant. Armless chairs fit easily around a dining table.*
Opposite: *Curved wooden arms on a low-to-the-floor chair were common in the Bauhaus period of the '30s in Europe. Moiré silk upholstery, a Chinese-red lamp shade, a wicker side table, and a wicker basket make a wonderful eclectic mix of styles, colors, and textures.*

Contemporary Wicker

Today's wicker furniture is no longer an exclusive industry; it covers a broad category in the home furnishings business. Many options are available to the consumer, from reproduction wicker to classic-style furniture to furniture with sleek, modern lines. Many current styles of woven furniture resemble standard furniture, sized and configured to service contemporary needs. Woven fibers are readily combined with exotic hardwood frames and upholstered cushions. The industry endlessly experiments with materials, shapes, colors, and functions to suit all life-styles, climates, and uses. The latest technology, improved construction methods, and new finishes have propelled wicker furniture into an exciting new era.

"The versatility of wicker and rattan combined with other natural materials, and different finishes, offers a

Left: The updated sweeping lines of this occasional chair are an overture to the Deco period. Rattan peel is woven like a refined fabric, draping the chair's ergonomic shape.
Opposite: Small side chairs like these serve many purposes. They can be used as dining room chairs, porch chairs, or extra chairs for company. These chairs would lighten up any room.

Top right: A zebra-like pattern is intricately woven with multicolors of fiber. Black leather braid trims the edge, the hardwood frame is made of stained mahogany, and the legs are carved to look like hooves. The upholstered seat is easily removed if a new fabric is desired. Bottom right: The use of color, material, and weave makes this chair an extraordinary example of the design freedom wicker allows. Opposite: The soft, pliable qualities of woven grass fibers act as an upholstery fabric on this overstuffed chair. Added is the undeniable elegance of leather cushions.

palette of creative options. It's like knitting a sweater. You change the color, the texture, and the thickness of the yarn, and you have a different look. It's the same with wicker and rattan. We strive to design with imagination to appeal to today's sophisticated consumer," says furniture designer Allan H. Palecek.

Woven furniture gives the designer a great opportunity to experiment with the use of fibers. Inventive combinations are endless. Braided sea grass, called double wall weave, covers wooden or rattan frames in such a way that the chair looks upholstered. Woven rattan peel is delicate and flexible enough to be used as an upholstery fabric. Abaca fiber can be plaited to resemble a cable-knit sweater. Flat strips of rattan are woven in a check pattern, herringbone design, or cross basket weave. Several shades of stained brown ropes are twisted together before weaving them into a beautiful armchair.

Rattan is the longest-used fiber in the industry, and designers are still finding infinite ways of using it. For example, a combination of Abaca fiber, rope, and leather are used to cover rattan frames, another way to bring added interest and texture to woven furniture. Peeled rattan is used when a stain is desired; skin-on rattan is used for natural texture and a brown color. Rattan legs on a sofa or chairs are bundled with leather strips. Rattan can be bleached and stained and used in a dual color weave to add interest and pattern. Franklin D. Roosevelt used rattan furniture in his USS *Potomac* home. The furniture was made of pencil-post rattan wrapped with reed. Palecek makes a very fine reproduction of FDR's ensemble.

Now, as in the early 1900s, a substantial portion of woven furniture is manufactured in Asian countries. Highly skilled craftsmen maintain a tradition of skills handed down through generations.

Left: A touch of the East Indies is reflected in the shape and design of this Ceylon Veranda chair from Bauer International. Down cushions make an afternoon of reading inviting.
Opposite: Woven of abaca fibers, this sofa and chair are complemented by the deep, rich color of mahogany legs. Cotton duck covers the down cushions.

Bauer International utilizes the craftsmanship of woven fibers in the East and West Indies for historic reference to British and Dutch colonies, which had a presence there in the late 1600s. Woven fibers add an interesting line to the furniture, providing a nice look and texture. Ken Bauer says, "I like the idea of it being a natural product, a natural medium that has soul to it." He

personally oversees the production of the furniture in his line. The fact that wicker was once a living root or vine gives the furniture an earthy quality. It's neither glossy nor high-tech looking. Woven furniture takes a traditional wood or upholstered chair, softens it up, and gives it natural elegance. "It's an art form . . . . You can see the craftsmanship of the people in the weaving of the chairs," Bauer says. Everything in the Bauer line is handwoven.

*Below left: The Plantation Long Chair is a look imported from exotic tropical countries. A durable wicker seat and cushioned headrest soften the solid wood frame, which is shaped to encourage a reclined position. **Below right:** This chair is not a reproduction of any vintage chair in the antique market. Completely new in shape and size, it has deep-set arms and a seat cushion that hugs the body, making this the perfect side chair in a formal living room. **Opposite:** Braided abaca fibers are alluringly new to the classic sleigh bed. The headboard is inviting to lean against while reading a book. Tropical plants and rattan wall coverings suggest a steamy bungalow in Java.*

Synthetic fibers are greatly improved from the past and are a practical alternative to natural fibers. Outdoor furniture made of UV-resistant plastic will withstand any weather condition. Furniture with a flared skirt, high rounded back, and tone-on-tone graphic—patterned after Art Deco period furniture—is now reproduced in plastic fibers as porch furniture. Its nostalgic look is appealing and also becomes practical in settings such as ski resorts, where it withstands harsh weather conditions. For a more tropical look, powder-coated metal chair frames are cast and colored to look like bamboo. The frames are combined with natural bamboo seats and backs, and the handsome furniture is practically indestructible. Special coloring techniques are used by

Above: Strictly Asian in design, this side chair, called the Singapore Sling Chair, is made up of a combination of wicker rattan and exotic plantation wood. The legs resemble the cabriole style first designed in the Victorian era. The modified curve is designed to add grace to the silhouette. *Opposite:* Gaming tables provided great social activities on safari or in Colonial social clubs. This exquisite version is designed to recapture the adventurous allure. Rattan wall coverings are rich in texture and natural beauty.

the Palecek furniture company to achieve a natural wicker-like appearance on charming UV-resistant plastic French Bistro chairs. The chic European look of this popular restaurant furniture translates well to the backyard patio and will last a lifetime.

3

Decorating with Wicker

There are no hard-and-fast rules that dictate what is right for interior decoration today. The multicultural makeup and rich history of the United States inspire many different styles and personal interpretations. Wicker also has a rich history in many different countries, and in that way can be considered truly American.

Wicker fits into grand rooms and humble ones, small, cozy rooms and stark, modern ones. Wicker can enhance a Victorian manor, a mission-style bungalow, a funky '50s ranch home, or a modern apartment. Individual tastes and whims can be met by different pieces of woven furniture. People want the ability to create personal spaces that reflect

Right: Romance, nostalgia, and the grace of soft, white colors is a way of life for Sue Balmforth of the antique shop Bountiful. Wicker furniture has a unique place in the interiors Balmforth masterfully puts together for the rich and famous. Left: The home of Will Rogers is made distinctive by stick wicker furniture similar to this sectional sofa. The canvas cushions and open weave frame give a sense of light and airiness.

Left: Lustrous sleek lines of a contemporary dining set are softened with wicker. Fiber woven in a box pattern is an inventive way to add texture to an otherwise austere chair. Combinations of materials inspire furniture designers to skillfully turn ideas into imaginative creations.
Opposite: Bar Harbor–style wicker is the single most popular style in woven furniture. The open weave was marketed for the first time in the 1950s. This reproduction ensemble is made broader and deeper than the originals to suit the contemporary figure. Note the cushioned ottoman that can also double as a coffee table.

PHOTO © PALECEK

individuality; they also want what is natural and comfortable. Interspersing wicker within any décor is more than an option; it is an opportunity to introduce old with new, texture with hard surface, color with basics, free-form shapes with classic ones. In addition, wicker furniture pieces are space savers—the perfect solution for small rooms.

Many vintage pieces of wicker furniture have no application in today's interiors. The function they once served is now obsolete and they are more interesting as collectibles. However, you can find creative ways to use these pieces. An antique baby buggy, for instance, can hold baby linens. An old sewing table can hold coasters, magazines, or remote controls. Wicker shelves can house a TV set and VCR tapes or a stereo system, CDs, and DVDs. With the current shabby-chic craze, wicker fits well into modern design, adding a touch of nostalgia to rooms.

There are few homes today that use entire ensembles of Victorian wicker furniture in their decor, but Victorian wicker is excellent used as accent pieces.

Intimate conversation areas enhanced by wicker armchairs and a small round table can create the perfect breakfast corner in a kitchen. The nostalgia of an old Victorian porch, furnished with a matching set of antique curlicue settees and chairs, is a great place to read a book, enjoy afternoon tea, or catch up with a neighbor who is walking by.

Nostalgia is the reason antique dealer Leslie Curtis opened one of the finest vintage wicker shops in the country. "My grandmother put wicker in her home," Curtis says. "She had wonderful taste and was able to integrate wicker into a formal sitting room. It always brings a little lightheartedness to an otherwise serious environment." This image so impressed Curtis as a young girl she began to study the use of wicker in other Victorian homes. That interest ultimately led to her passion for collecting and selling wicker. "In my home, the guest rooms were very formal. I had two stepdaughters who would visit periodically. I wanted a more playful atmosphere for them so I furnished the guest

PHOTO © MARY WHITESIDES

The nostalgia of an old country home looks fresh and updated with the use of bright colors. The owners of Wild Goose Chase antiques in Orange County believe in refreshing antique wicker with unusual colors. The painting of an old luxury liner adds to the period flavor of the room.

The use of stick wicker in this southwestern-style living room is testament to the versatility of wicker furniture. Martin Kuckly of Kuckly Associates uses reproduction stick wicker in honor of the 1930s limited editions. The Will Rogers Library is one of the best examples of how stick wicker was used in a western application.

rooms in vintage wicker." Curtis considers American wicker the best quality in the world. The golden years of the wicker age set the standards for sturdy hardwood frames and the finest rattan overlay.

One doesn't need to live in a Victorian home to enjoy the whimsy of an artistic wicker chair. Today Victorian wicker is used in a variety of settings. The owner of a beautiful Park Avenue penthouse invigorates her space with a rare woven chair. She is a lover of art and considers the chair an addition to her collection. Some people want something more traditional like the open weave of Bar Harbor wicker that reminds them of summertime in the Hamptons. Bar Harbor furniture played an important role in the evolution of the Arts and Crafts movement.

Bungalow-style homes of the mission period are enjoying a renewed interest among homeowners; first-time owners are buying and renovating the original structures of the '30s. In addition,

Chairs woven from sea grass suit this Asian-style dining room. Sea grass grows prolifically in Asian countries. The large, spongy fibers, which are soft and forgiving, are traditionally woven in a braided pattern. Because of its flexibility, it can be used as upholstery fabric would be.

designers and builders are interpreting the mission style in newly built homes.

The quality and clean lines of the Arts and Crafts movement suggest an abundant use of quartersawn oak and Stickley furnishings. The hard-edge appearance of oak tables and chairs, wooden wainscoting, and dark oak cabinets can be softened with the use of authentic wicker from the 1920s and '30s. The earthen colors and notorious diamond design stained on a chair back adds a casual element to an otherwise austere environment.

Below: A modern version of the romantic look is accented by a clean line wooden chair that is softened by a painted sea grass back. Contrasting colors, cushions, and flowers accent the purity of white tones. Woven materials are an excellent way to add softness, texture, and warmth to a space. *Opposite:* This Mandalay console table has the look of small, square drawers, even though the actual drawers are large and roomy. Woven rattan peel is applied to solid wood for texture and natural appeal. This is a perfect piece for storing table linens, flatware, and napkin rings.

Decorating with Wicker **95**

For a softer, more formal elegance, Leslie Curtis of Curtis Antiques

reproduces a wicker version of the famous Eames Chair. Every detail of the

chair is handcrafted, down to the simple peg-and-notch reclining mechanism

behind the chair back. The caramel colored, stained rattan is a luscious com-

plement to the dark hard-edge lines of mission furniture. Earth-toned wicker pieces placed throughout Arts & Crafts–style interiors add distinct character, a soothing presence, and textural interest.

The 1930s and '40s early stick furniture is a rare find. This type of furniture was not around very long, so the pieces are limited and valuable. If dark stained rattan chairs with earth-tone fabrics can be found, they look great in a library, home office, or sitting room. Stick furniture upholstered in Indian trading blanket fabric looks great in mission-style interiors. The subtle, simple lines and medium-weight pole construction of stick furniture fits with a mix of antique furniture from different periods. These rare rattan pieces can be upholstered with any number of patterns that will change them into an ensemble to complement any interior. A reproduction of the rare stick furniture, called the President's Collection, is reproduced by the Palecek Company. Very much like the vintage ensemble found in the Will Rogers library, this set is brought forward into a contemporary setting with plain ecru velvet cushions.

Right: This small-scale wicker chair is an excellent choice for tight spaces. The extra pole framing supports the arms, and the high back provides support for head and neck. The antique paint finish is reminiscent of the Karpin Furniture Company wipe-off process. Opposite: Bent willow is a western-grown fiber that is decidedly rustic in look and feel. Willow is bent and shaped much like rattan pole, but has a look all its own. The bark is left intact, and branches cut from the surface leave a polka-dot effect.

PHOTO © MARY WHITESIDES

As much as earth-toned wicker defines the mission period, bright colors and funky shapes define the 1950s rattan furniture. The bold botanical fabrics and hefty rattan frames suggest a tropical theme; this playful look of authentic rattan furniture is a natural for a home on the beach or a theme room in a New York apartment. However, in nontropical areas, it is generally difficult to integrate this type of pole rattan furniture into another mix of furniture. For a different look, stain the pole frame dark and upholster the cushions in a mohair velvet or Art Deco printed velvet. Place two armchairs astride a side table and include this funky look in an informal living room with overstuffed sofas.

Exotic, adventurous, practical, interesting, and artistic all define the contemporary woven furniture available today. The wide assortment of styles, colors, weaves, and combinations of

An updated version of an antique chair called the Snowshoe, these chairs and the table can be tucked into a corner, added to an entrance with limited space, or used in a garden, patio, or porch setting. The dark stain adds richness, while the cane backs add texture.

PHOTO © PALECEK

materials suits many different tastes and interior design styles. Choose from any theme and create a fantasy room. Perhaps the adventures of the Stiles Bros. on African Safari sparks your imagination; the old steamer trunks they used on their voyages have been interpreted in a line of furniture by Bauer International. Woven cane is paired with leather, brass, and wood. The furniture line includes tables that look like trunks and jungle safari baskets with leather lids. If you prefer, furniture of sea grass, abaca, and reed paired with solid mahogany and leather accents can give a room an East or West Indies flair. A number of combinations can transform a bedroom into the style of world traveler–adventurer.

The ingenious Hunt Club Chair from the Bauer line combines the texture

---

Above: A pole rattan frame is covered with a double wall of woven sea grass. Sea grass is known for its durability and flexibility. This contemporary chair is a refreshing sculptural shape and suits the look of several interior styles. In this application, it is paired with an Asian chest. **Opposite:** A lap pool looks like an elegant water feature in a grand sports lounge. Oversized wicker chairs easily seat two people or give plenty of room for someone who wants to spread out after a few laps.

of woven furniture with leather cushions, making a comfortable overstuffed chair. The earthy quality of the chair will fit into almost any style interior you choose. This chair is especially nice in a mountain home or a western lodge.

The classic lines of the Bridgeport Collection from the Palecek Company honor the popular furniture of the early 1900s. With large dimensions, this collection is suitable for the living room. The pitch of the seat has been maximized for comfort. These reproductions have a fresh look and yet evoke the nostalgia of the original antiques.

Below: *A combination of materials allows a designer the freedom and medium for a new look in furniture. This grouping is a good example. The furniture is constructed of plantation hardwood with a hand-rubbed finish. The luxury of leather is a smooth contrast to the hand-woven sea grass in a herringbone pattern. Comfort is assured by careful consideration to the size, shape, and plush lines of the upholstery.* ***Opposite:*** *The constant humidity on a yacht can have a debilitating effect on wooden furniture. Wicker furniture is an excellent choice in these conditions as it is refreshed, rather than worn down, by moisture.*

PHOTO © PALECEK

Sleek, contemporary lines give a clean, uncluttered look to an interior. Free-form woven furniture is an artistic option for a modern setting. The artisans in Colombia experiment with new, modern shapes for woven furniture. Clean and refreshing, the simple boxy lines of a sofa and chair are softened by upholstered cushions. The inventive idea that bench and coffee table can be combined is carried out by the designers in Colombia: a wicker coffee table bench is created with a flat table surface between two cushions.

The exciting and endless possibilities for woven furniture reach into the past and continue into the future. Weaving furniture is older than any craft in the history of art. Woven furniture can personalize a home in endless ways; consider the choice of wicker furniture an opportunity to individualize a nook or cranny, a simple room, or the entire house.

4

Accessorizing
with Wicker

Wicker was first used in making baskets. Examples of baskets are mentioned in the Bible, illustrated on ancient walls in Syria and Egypt, and have been used for centuries to gather harvests in China. From ancient times to modern, woven baskets have been the most practical domestic product ever to be invented and are used in every way imaginable. Whether found in a mansion or a humble bungalow, wicker baskets have a place and a function in the home.

Wicker baskets range from plain and sturdy to ornate, and can

 PHOTO © BAUER INTERNATIONAL, INC.

Opposite: Good interior design is filled with contrasts. Here, woven accessories lighten an ornately carved wooden chest. The wicker takes the formality out of an otherwise ceremonious console.
Right: This large basket is actually a sturdy storage table. It sits on a solid wood base and has a dual-tone antique finish.

be delicate works of art. Baskets are great organizers for the home. They come in all sizes, shapes, colors, materials, and styles. Wicker baskets are lightweight, inexpensive, and easy to clean; they can add a note of drama or whimsy to the home. Unlike plastic containers, they are earthy, warm, tactile, and beautiful. Baskets are made from a variety of materials including sea grass, rattan pole, peeled rattan, rope, sea pods, willow, banana leaves, and coconut

twigs. All finishes on baskets used for produce are made food safe. Wicker containers used for heavy lifting, or to support plants in pots, are generally constructed with a wooden base for strength. When searching for a basket to perform a specific task, be sure the construction is compatible with your requirements. Choosing the right basket for the right function is the key to maximizing their utility.

Consider the style of your home when choosing baskets. Baskets with sleek lines made of refined, intricately woven materials suit a contemporary home. Dark, richly colored baskets with combinations of materials suit a rustic-style home. Fabric-lined baskets and baskets with handles in natural rattan (known as the classics) look right in a country-style home. For an Arts & Crafts home, choose bold, waffle-weave baskets made of flat banana leaves and stained with intense colors such as red, green, or black. The index of choices really is endless. No matter what your style is, finding the perfect basket for your home can be fun and satisfying.

Opposite: Baskets come in all sizes, shapes, and colors, with and without lids, handles, and liners. This is a selection of beautifully crafted storage baskets, lidded in leather.
Right: A basket is perfect for an arrangement of silk or dried flowers or to hold a ceramic planter.

*Left: Canvas-lined baskets serve a utilitarian purpose unlike any other hamper. The convenience of carrying laundry to the washer is made easy by simply removing and cinching the bag. **Above:** The beauty of a twisted bronze handle on a wicker magazine rack is enhanced by green bottle glass.*

Organizing with Baskets

The wicker basket is a taskmaster for any room in the house. Take stock of the needs in a given area, weigh the clutter issue, note the space available, and then determine the kind and size of basket that will solve the problem.

Entryways & Mud Rooms • A large, deep basket can collect muddy shoes and minimize dirt carried into the house. It's also a great way to eliminate that pile of shoes you keep stumbling over. A square basket with a lid will hide mittens, hats, and scarves. Clutter is gone in an instant. If the baskets get dirty, they are easily cleaned. Just take them outside and hose them down.

Living Rooms & Family Rooms • Baskets in the living room and family room are a quick fix for newspaper and magazine clutter. Decide whether to stack magazines in a deep basket, stand them in a large square basket with handles, or hide them completely in a lidded basket. The construction of the basket should be sturdy enough to withstand the weight of the magazines. *TV Guides*, remote controls, and coasters are easily found when placed in a designated basket. Some baskets have sectioned spaces to organize such small items as pencils, notepads, and cocktail napkins.

Bathrooms • Limited space in the bathroom may be a problem. If you don't have shelf or closet space for towels, roll them and organize them in a wicker basket that you place on the floor or countertop. Not only does this provide extra storage space, but it adds design dimension to the room. Baskets arranged on shelves provide an organizational

PHOTO © DEBRA MACFARLANE, BOUNTIFUL

Right: Sue Balmforth of Bountiful organizes guest towels by rolling them and beautifully presenting them in a wicker basket.

tool for various toiletry items, as well as adding charm and romantic appeal to the room. Eradicate the embarrassment of running out of toilet paper, especially in the guest bath, by placing an extra roll in a basket placed on the toilet tank. Reading material can be discreetly located in a wicker container near the toilet. Provide a hamper in the bathroom to keep used towels off the floor.

Bedrooms • Assign family members their own set of baskets for organization. Children, for instance, could have a toy basket or a homework basket. Nothing can conceal the clutter of toys more easily than a series of toy baskets on a shelf. It is easy and fun for children to pick up toys when the container personalizes their possessions. Older children can organize their books, notebooks, homework papers, and pencils in a basket much as a home office would be. This is a good opportunity to train a child in the organizational necessities of a working office. The frustration of misplaced school papers and

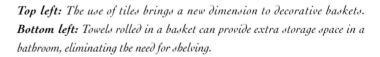

Top left: The use of tiles brings a new dimension to decorative baskets. Bottom left: Towels rolled in a basket can provide extra storage space in a bathroom, eliminating the need for shelving.

A series of precisely woven square boxes is useful in a home office or as a catchall in the bedroom. The beauty of bamboo handles contrasts with the flat banana fibers dyed in bright colors.

supplies will decrease when wicker trays, boxes, and pencil holders are used. Many baskets come with slot handles woven into the pattern, or wooden or metal handles. Lightweight baskets with handles are easy for kids to carry.

Clothing can be organized with wicker accessories for all members of the family. A personal, lined clothes basket encourages neatness. Once the basket is filled with dirty clothes, the liner can simply be carried to the laundry room. With a square lined basket for folded clothes, members of the family can pick up their own laundered clothing and carry it back to their rooms. They can return it to drawers, or, if these baskets act as drawers on shelves, clothes are automatically put away.

Also consider a small basket on the nightstand for reading glasses, books, sticky notes, and pens. And, of course, wicker wastepaper baskets make stylish containers and help you keep the room clean.

Top left: Twisted metal along the edges of this oblong basket provides a graceful handle to carry bread from counter to table.
Bottom left: A series of three stacked baskets are shaped like a shallow bowl. Wicker containers are perfect for fruit because the open nature of woven fiber keeps produce fresh.

Kitchens • The most common place in the house for woven containers is the kitchen, and wicker accessories can be used endlessly in this setting. The old expression "bread basket" came about for good reason—the sculptural beauty of a gourmet loaf of bread is given the regard it deserves when displayed in an artistic basket. A decorative basket used as a centerpiece may hold fresh white napkins, extra candles, or napkin rings. Or you can keep three or four baskets of small, nonperishable treats on kitchen counters.

Nothing connotes abundance more than an artistic display of fresh fruit. Fresh fruit in a basket entices one to nibble in a healthy way. In addition, fruit can breathe easily through the airy weave of a basket, preventing mold and brown spots. Produce such as potatoes and onions do well in wicker baskets on kitchen shelves. Small wicker containers are also a nice way to organize recipes and shopping lists.

Household cleaning products stored in wicker baskets beneath the sink are ready totes that can be carried to any spot in the house. A basket left at the foot of a staircase is a handy way to collect stray clutter.

Lampshades

The current selection of wicker lampshades is a far cry from the simple, trite hanging shades of the past. New shades range from round to square, rectangular, fluted, and scalloped. They come in colors like sea grass, bark, tan, and natural, as well as bold colors such as red, green, and blue. A wide range of lamp bases adds to the whimsy of a woven shade. Sculptural metal bases can take on all kinds of plant and tree forms and are nicely complemented by a wicker shade. Shades with patterns of flowers work well in a garden room or breakfast area, while the sweeping conical shape of a bamboo shade on a wooden base adds an oriental touch to a room such as a library or den.

A sweeping cone shape made of rattan peel gives this lampshade an oriental touch.

PHOTO © PALECEK

118 Wicker Design

Other Accessories

Other options for accessorizing with wicker include room screens, footstools, plant stands, storage tables, magazine racks, and even vases. Choose a room screen of woven sea grass to define and soften the corner of a room. The drama of a 48-inch high, intricately woven rope vase in an elegant silhouette is a great space filler in an entrance. Magazine racks are standard home furnishing items in any home. Reading material can be decoratively housed in a wicker stand with an iron frame and handle. Wicker footstools are lightweight, handy, and easily moved from chair to chair or room to room.

Opposite: Wicker shades are a far cry from the round baskets used as hanging lamps in the '60s. The texture of woven fiber is an ideal way to filter a pleasing stream of light. This lamp base is trimmed with winsome branches of wisteria made of metal and glass. Right: Standing sixty inches high, this Havana floor lamp is loosely woven to filter a soft, moody light into a room.

The use of wicker throughout the house offers great design solutions and provides a comprehensive response to common household clutter. The liberating feeling of well-organized living spaces, and home furnishing accessories with texture and warmth made from nature's gifts, are achieved with flare and good taste by the oldest craft in history—the woven craft of wicker.

Right: A giant urn woven of rope is an exquisite choice for an entrance. *Below:* This handy footstool can be moved from chair to chair or room to room. *Opposite:* This unique picnic set is fashioned after the old steamer trunks taken on African safaris. Manufactured by Bauer International, Inc.

PHOTOS © PALECEK

122   Wicker Design

Above: *Using wicker as his medium, an artisan in Colombia makes whimsical animals. The donkey in the upper left corner is really a basket that can be used for pencils, napkins, or candles. The turtle in the upper right corner is great in the bathroom for toiletries. The peacock and the chicken are accessories for the kitchen.* *Opposite:* *Room screens are great space dividers and excellent for defining the corner of a room. This simple, metal frame is softened by the braided texture of sea grass.*

5

How to Care for Your Wicker

When good quality materials are used and the vines are woven properly, wicker should last a hundred years or more with normal use. Hundreds of antique wicker pieces are still in use today. Wicker's durability comes from the properties of the material. A rattan vine, which can be cut into various widths and shapes, is filled with fibers running lengthwise, giving it the strength of multistrand cable. A vine will bend, but—unlike wood—it will not splinter or break. Many, who are accustomed to wood furniture,

PHOTO © MARY WHITESIDES

Left: A formal dining room is offset by a garden room. The casual attraction of wicker furniture invites one to relax after a fine meal, to read a book, or enjoy the flowers.
Above: A simple picnic basket brings with it the nostalgia of a leisurely meal under a tree. A wood structure on this wicker basket provides a solid base to stabilize the woven material. This particular basket has been refreshed with a coat of paint. From Wild Goose Chase in Orange County, California.

Above left: Painting wicker furniture black was a bold move on the part of the manufacturer. Consumers had already taken the step to update their old pieces of wicker after World War II. Above right: Antique painted pieces have often been painted with many layers over the years. As layers of paint flake off, they expose another color beneath the top coat. A white chip paint piece such as the one pictured here is difficult to find and highly valued by interior designers. Opposite: Original Bar Harbor wicker chairs like these are a rare find. Sue Balmforth shops the country for her store Bountiful in Los Angeles.

mistake wicker's flexibility for weakness. The weaving of fiber on fiber reinforces the material, giving added strength far beyond the single fiber.

Consider the kind of wicker you own as well as its finish to determine the type of care and maintenance it needs. Is your wicker made of natural rattan, willows, or reeds? Is it made of sea grass, paper-wrapped wire, or raffia? What about the finish? Is it lacquered, oiled, stained, or painted? Contemporary outdoor wicker is often made of acrylic, nylon, or plastic fibers. Each type of fiber requires special care specific to the properties of the material.

Cleaning Your Wicker

The way in which you clean your wicker is very different depending on the materials from which it is made. The following information will help you properly clean and maintain your wicker.

Natural Wicker • Wicker should be cleaned regularly to maintain the color and pliability of the material. Always vacuum loose dirt and go over the wicker with a sponge dampened with water and detergent. Rinse with a garden hose, but be careful not to soak any wood that may be part of the furniture. Soaking the wicker fibers with a hose, however, can soften natural fibers that have turned brittle. Dry quickly in the sun or use a fan or hair dryer. Wait several days before using the furniture. If there are sharp or fuzzy strands, sand with fine sandpaper to smooth them out. If the wicker is cracked, give it a coat of boiled linseed oil (available at art supply stores) applied by brush. Cracking in wicker is caused by excessive dryness and applying lacquer or varnish will make it brittle. Linseed oil will replenish the reed and

PHOTO © DEBRA MACFARLANE, BOUNTIFUL

cure to a hard finish. If the wicker dries to be dull looking, give it another coat. This is an indication that the reed is very dry. Use rags or paper towels to remove excess oil and a dry brush to get into the cracks and crevices. Do not put Polyurethane on wicker—it will cause further cracking. Unpainted wicker rubbed with linseed oil will enhance and deepen the natural color. Dispose of soaked rags as per instructions on the can. They can be combustible.

Below: Furniture used on a patio, porch, or in a garden is assaulted by the sun, rain, and wind. To minimize the effort of having to constantly move, cover, or store outdoor furniture, the manufacturer has come up with a plastic fiber woven in the same manner as wicker. These pieces are handsome and practical and can be left out year-round.
Opposite: *Painting a wicker chair can personalize your home. This particular chair, although an antique, has been recently painted by the Heidemanns of Wild Goose Chase antiques.*

Painted or Lacquered Wicker •

Brush the wicker with a dry, soft-bristle brush to loosen dirt. If paint is flaking, lightly sand and touch up with matching paint. The paint finish can also be sealed with thinned lacquer. Wipe painted wicker with a soapy sponge and rinse with a wet sponge. Blot with a towel and allow it to dry in the sun. Spraying painted wicker with a hose may cause further paint chipping and cracking.

Note: Many antique wicker collectors highly value old pieces with chipped white paint. In this case, do not attempt to restore the paint. Instead, vacuum or carefully wipe the wicker surface frequently. Further flaking may occur but that is the beauty of this type wicker.

PHOTO © MARY WHITESIDES

Stained Wicker • Vacuum and wipe with a damp cloth. To remove dirt from hard-to-reach cracks, use a toothbrush. Do not spray with the hose or rinse with water as stains on wicker, unless sealed, will diffuse with water. Do not leave stained wicker in direct sunlight as it will fade. To enhance colors and increase pliability, spray with a light oil and dab off the excess with a soft cloth. This type of wicker can be easily refreshed with a new coat of stain. Some rare antique pieces are stained in multiple colors, making restoration a time-consuming nightmare.

Sea Grass, Paper-Wrapped Wire, Raffia • Cleaning these natural fibers with water will cause them to disintegrate. Brushing will cause ripping and loosening of fibers, and will eventually break the piece down altogether. Although these fibers are durable and can last a long time, they need special handling. Wipe furniture made of grass or raffia gently with oiled cloths to maintain pliability. Wipe furniture made of paper-wrapped wire with a soft moist cloth. Paper is too absorbent to use any kind of oil. You can lightly vacuum grass and paper furniture with a soft-bristle brush to remove dust from deep cracks. Keep this type of furniture out of direct sunlight and away from heat ventilators.

Painting Your Wicker

Serious collectors of antique wicker think it is a crime to paint wicker. The most valued wicker of the late 1800s and early 1900s is natural wicker. Wicker didn't originally come out of the factories painted; consumers started the craze by painting their own furniture to suit a color scheme or decorating theme. The factories did eventually follow suit, however, and there are examples of painted wicker from quite early on.

If you get a piece of over-painted wicker that is chipped, you might be able to see the different colors of paint from the different layers. Based on paint colors, you can go through the periods of time from the early 1900s. The colors are distinctly representative of the period. A few early twentieth century pieces were painted black. In the late 1920s, you can find a range of colors, including greens, reds, blues, and ochre. Orange and apple green were popular in the '50s.

Painting your own color scheme on a piece of wicker is quite easy to achieve. The following is needed to paint wicker: A drop cloth, sponge, vegetable oil, soapy water, liquid deglosser, and spray acrylic paint. First prepare the surface to be painted by sponge cleaning with soapy water. Next use a liquid deglosser to dull the surface so the paint will adhere. Be sure you choose an open area in which to paint. Spray the first coat very lightly and don't worry too much about coverage on the first pass. It is important to prevent drips and running. Spray a second coat and let dry. If the coverage is not sufficient, spray one more time. Be sure to spray at different angles to insure proper coverage. For an antique paint finish, wipe the surface of the paint after it partially dries to expose the natural wicker.

This wicker chair awaits a finalized color choice. It will be spray painted to adequately cover the surface and cracks. (See the process of this chair being woven on page 21.)

Staining Your Wicker

After World War II, natural piece wicker was often stained and the shellac in the crevices darkened. Examples of vintage stain colors can be found in old Heywood Wakefield pieces. The look of that antique wicker is popular today. It is fairly easy to achieve the worn look.

To individualize your wicker furniture, consider staining it. The process is simple. Natural wicker can be purchased for economical prices at places like Pier 1; stains are available in many different colors. Once the furniture and color of stain are chosen, you will need the following: a drop cloth, several sponge brushes, soft cloths or paper towels, a sponge, and a hair dryer. Work in an open area. Apply a liberal amount of stain to the wicker with a sponge brush, making sure to get a good amount of stain in the crevices. Wipe drips immediately. With a hair dryer, blow the stain into crevices. Immediately wipe the surface with the sponge to remove some of the stain. The result should be a darker tone in the crevices and lighter tones on the surface. Allow the furniture to dry overnight.

*Top right: Synthetic bright red wicker will never need to be refurbished. The permanent color will withstand weather and constant wear. This is an example of a vintage style used in a contemporary setting. **Bottom right:** This handsome and inviting outdoor rocking chair is a practical, all-weather version of natural fiber wicker. The bold stripe cushions add a bright design element to the mute tones of the chair.*

ANDY GOLDSWORTHY

Resources

INTERIOR DESIGNERS &
ARCHITECTS

Howard Backan
Backan Gillam Architects
2352 Marinship Way
Sausalito, CA 94965
Phone: (415) 289–3860
Fax: (415) 289–3866
www.bgarch.com

Leslie Curtis
8252 Melrose Ave.
Los Angeles, CA 90046
Phone: (323) 653–2999
Fax: (323) 653–0620

Kuckly Associates
Martin Kuckly
68 Main St.
Irvington, NY 10533
Phone: (914) 479–1700

Lifestyle Interior Decorating
Virginia Goshe
1721 Maple Leaf Blvd.
Oldsmar, FL 34677
Phone: (727) 488–1698
Fax: (813) 891–1058

Gina Robinson
Phone: (310) 453–0701
Fax: (310) 721–4386

WICKER AND RATTAN

The Agoura Antique Mart
Maria & David Bartolet
28863 Agoura Rd.
Agoura Hills, CA 91301
Phone: (818) 706–8366
Fax: (818) 706–1508

The American Wing
2415 Montauk Hwy.
Bridgehampton, NY 11932
Phone: (631) 537–3319
Fax: (631) 537–3339

Antique Depot
155 S. Glassell
Orange, CA 92866
Phone: (714) 516–1731
Fax: (714) 516–1849

Antiques on Fair Oaks
Francesca de la Flor
Roy Aldridge
330 S. Fair Oaks Ave.
Pasadena, CA 91105
Phone: (626) 449–9590
Fax: (626) 449–9441
www.antiquesonfairoaks.com

Artesanias de Colombia
Carrera 3a
No. 18A–58
www.comerci@colomsat.net.co

Artifacts Trading Company, Inc.
Phone: (312) 850–0041
Rattan only

Bali Art
www.baliartsacc.com

Bali Exports Co.
Bayod Kedisan
Tegallalang-Gianyar, Bali 80361
Indonesia
Fax (62) 361–765969
www.baliexports.com

———

PHOTO © MARY WHITESIDES

North American Office
Mr. Len Fridman
PO Box 429
Danfort Unit 503
Toronto, ON M4K 1P1
Phone: (416) 418–1059
lenfridman@baliexport.com

Bauer International, Inc.
Ken Bauer
414 Jessen Ln.
Wando, SC 29492
Phone: (843) 884–4007
Fax: (843) 884–7789
www.bauerinternational.com

BIMA
Autopipsta Norte
No. 232–35
Local 4–112
Bogota, Colombia
Phone: 236 68 37
www.chumbis@hotmail.com

Bountiful
Sue Balmforth
1335 Abbot Kinney Blvd.
Venice, CA 90291
Phone: (310) 450–3620
Fax: (310) 314–8231

Campo
Brian Seethaler
2855 South Highland Dr.
Salt Lake City, UT 84106
Phone: (801) 474–1240
Fax: (801) 474–1241

Chesapeake
www.chesapeake.net

Cheshire Cat Antique Mall
Lynn Wilson
671 Fir St.
Qualicum Beach, BC V9K 1T4
Phone / Fax: (250) 752–2142
lynn@cheshirecatantique.ca

Coco Co.
363 W. Erie #2E
Chicago, IL 60610
Phone: (312) 915–0043
Fax: (312) 915–5933
Cococorp@aol.com

Country Roads Antiques & Gardens
Sue Jackson
204 W. Chapman
Orange, CA 92866
Phone: (714) 532–3041
Fax: (714) 532–2492
www.countryroadsantiques.com

Karen Crane's
La Dee Da Antique Centre
28859 West Agoura Rd.
Agoura Hills, CA 91301
Phone: (818) 879–8698
Fax: (818) 879–8275

Leslie Curtis Antiques & Design
Leslie Curtis
8253 Melrose Ave.
Los Angeles, CA 90046
Phone: (323) 653–2999
Fax: (323) 653–0620

Cape Cod Office
Route 6A
PO Box 1013
Dennis, MA 02638
Phone: (508) 385–2921

Digs
Michele Novak
1340 Abbot Kinney Blvd.
Venice, CA 90291
Phone: (310) 450–3072
Fax: (310) 450–6498
www.digshome.com

Dovetail Antiques
Peter and Susan Tanzini
474 White Pine Rd.
Columbus, NJ 08022
Phone: (609) 298–5245
Fax: (609) 298–1229
www.dovetailantiquewicker.com

Lloyd Flanders
Wicker at Leisure Home Center
3420 Mall Dr.
Eau Claire, WI 54701

Frans Wicker
295 Route 10 E
Succasunna, NJ 07876
Phone: (800) 372–6799
www.franswicker.com

E.L. Higgins
PO Box 69
Bernard, ME 04612
Phone: (207) 244–3983
info@antiquewicker.com
www.antiquewicker.com

Newport Avenue Antique Center
4864 Newport Ave.
San Diego, CA 92107
Phone: (619) 222–8686
Fax: (619) 222–1485

Palecek
Darcy Forman, Representative
17517 E. San Marcus Dr.
Fountain Hills, AZ 85268
Phone: (480) 837–5205
Fax: (480) 837–5211

Main Office
Phone: (800) 274–7730
Fax: (510) 238–7234

Pavilion Rattan Ltd.
Modern Shapes
Phone: 44 (0) 1623–811–343
Fax: 44 (0) 1623–810–123
sales@pavilionrattan.co.uk
www.pavilionrattan.co.uk

Pier 1 Imports
Phone: (800) 447–4371
www.pier1.com

The Rattan Shoppe
2049 Yonge St.
Toronto, ON M4S 2A2
Phone: (416) 486–1373
(888) 479–6186
Fax: (416) 486–1386

Maxine & Henry Speski
Connecticut Antique Wicker
97 Copper Beech Drive
Rocky Hill, CT 06067
Phone: (860) 721–7781
By appointment
Specializes in vintage wicker

Victory Furniture
9040 W. Pico Blvd.
Los Angeles, CA 90035
Phone: (310) 276–4272
Fax: (310) 276–3572
victory800@aol.com

Vintage Rattan
PO Box 34
Hartford, MI 49057
info@springdalefurnishings.com
www.springdalefurnishings.com

Wicker Rattan Imports
1050 RT 46
Ledgewood, NJ 07853
Phone: (973) 927–8530
Fax: (973) 584–7446
www.dfwicker.com

The Wicker Shop of Maine
US Route #1
Wells, ME 04090
Phone: (207) 646–8555
wickerlady@thewickershop.com
www.thewickershop.com

The Wicker Tree
308 Springfield Ave.
Summit, NJ 07901
Phone: (908) 273–4030
Fax: (908) 273–3037

Wicker Works
Box 169
Gooderham, ON K0M 1R0
Phone: (705) 447–2435
Fax: (705) 447–2433
www.wickerworks.on.ca

Wickerland
6125 Centre St. SW
Calgary, AB T2H 0C5
Phone: (403) 258–2506
www.wickerlandcanada.com

Wicker World
120 McPhillips St.
Winnepeg, MB R3E 2J7
Phone: (204) 770–2900
www.info@wicker-world.com

Wild Goose Chase
Bill Heidemann
Antique Americana & Interiors
105 West Chapman Ave.
Orange, CA 92866
Phone: (714) 532–6807

Yesteryear Wicker
7616 Investment Court
Owings, MD 20736
Phone: (410) 257–1302
Fax: (410) 257–1306
infor@yesteryearwicker.com
www.yesteryearwicker.com

For a comprehensive selection of
wicker online:
www.caneonline.co.uk
Phone: 01349895013

BASKETS

Bauer International
414 Jessen Lane
Wando, SC 29492
Phone: (843) 884–4007
Fax: (843) 884–7789
www.bauerinternational.com

Black Ash Shaker Baskets
Robert M. Gelinas
PO Box 106
Farmington, NH 93835
Phone: (603) 755–2119
basb@tias.com

Bodacious Baskets
1022 Goss Ave.
Menasha, WI 54952
Phone: (920) 830–0051
info@bodaciousbasketry.com

Bountiful Baskets
155 Edens Lane
Florence, MT 59833
Phone: (406) 273–6120
www.antb.com

Homegoods #246
Pride Center
22940 Victory Blvd.
Woodland Hills, CA 91367
Phone: (818) 348–1722
(800) 888–0776
www.homegoodsinc@tjx.com

Palecek
Darcy Forman
17517 E. San Marcus Drive
Fountain Hills, AZ 85268
Phone: (480) 837–5205
(800) 274–7730
Fax: (480) 837–5211

Simply Baskets
Kathleen Becker
3965 Bellingrath Main N.W.
Kennesaw, GA 30144-6020
Phone: (770) 426–6253
www.rubylane.com

Bibliography

Classic Wicker Furniture: The Complete Illustrated Catalog, 1898-1899. Heywood

Brothers and Wakefield Company, 1982.

Meschi, Bob. *Antique Wicker from the Heywood Wakefield Catalog.* Schiffer, 1994.

Saunders, Richard. *The Official Price Guide to Wicker,* 3rd Edition. Crown

Publisher, 1985.

Saunders, Richard. *Wicker Furniture: A Guide to Restoring and Collecting.* Crown

Publisher, 1990.

Scott, Tim. *Fine Wicker Furniture, 1870-1930.* Schiffer, 1990.